This book is dedicated to the kids of the Nexus Fighter Academy, and specially my daughters Gisele, Anais and Carla. They are an amazing team of funny, tireless, hard working little fight monsters, without whom I wouldn't be coaching youth sports or writing children's books.

TABLE OF CONTENTS

Table of contents 3
Introduction 4
The ruleset 5
The competition area 6
The referee 8
The competion Gi 9
Hygiene 10
Common ways to win 12
    Submission 12
    Stoppage 14
    Winning by points 16
    Referee decision 18
    Disqualification 20
The score system 22
    Takedown 23
    Guard pass 24
    Mount and back-mount 26
    Back-take 27
    Sweep 28
Advantages 30
Fouls 31
    Disciplinary fouls 31
    Serious fouls 32
    Severe fouls 34
Aknowledgements 37
Learning activities 39
About the author and the illustrator 49

INTRODUCTION

Hey there, how are you?

If you are reading this book it is because you are a Brazilian Jiu Jitsu athlete or, as we prefer to call ourselves, a **BJJ fighter**. That's a much cooler name, isn't it?!

Maybe you started this sport not too long ago, or maybe you are one of those advanced kids in the gym that helps the trainer with the younger members. Maybe you are even already a competitor yourself!

Whether you are new to the sport or have been training for years, BJJ is a fun and rewarding sport for people of all levels. Not only is it a lot of **fun**, but you are also becoming faster, stronger, and more confident. You are learning how to defend yourself, and how to fight. Isn't BJJ the best?!

To create a good environment to train, there needs to be some basic rules that everyone agrees to follow. These keep training and competitions safe, fair, and allow room for improvement.

You probably already know that kicking and striking is not allowed. Those are easy things to remember! But what about the trickier things like points and fouls? Do you know how many points you receive for each technique? Who wins the match when time runs out and neither fighter has been submitted? Which techniques you're not allowed to use and which might cause a foul?

THE RULESET

This book will explain the most important rules of **Brazilian Jiu Jitsu** in clear and easy terms. If you are a competitor, having this knowledge can make a big difference in helping you win your match!

If you are the parent or friend of a BJJ fighter, this book will be very helpful for you too. It's not uncommon to see spectators looking confused while attending a **competition!** But, when you understand the basic rules, you can easily follow along with what's happening in a match and will be much better able to encourage and support your BJJ fighter!

Before we begin, just a few last words. One of the amazing things about BJJ is that there are fighters and competitions all around the world! But beware: not all of the competitions follow the same set of rules.

In this book, we explain the set of rules that are the most commonly used worldwide: the IBJJF rules. These were created by the International Brazilian Jiu Jitsu Federation (IBJJF).

The entire official IBJJF set of **rules** includes details for many very specific situations. Instead of trying to cover every single detail, this book will summarize only the most important rules, the ones you are most likely to use and see in a competition.

If you want to learn more about the IBJJF rules, you can download the complete rule book from their website at www.ibjjf.org for free. They're a little more challenging to read, but if you're eager to learn, with a little patience and practice, I'm confident you can understand these as well!

THE COMPETITION AREA

You have finally arrived at the competition hall. Hurray! You are very **brave**. Just by showing up you have proved to yourself and to all others that you are a real champion. What do you notice as you look around?

The seats are full of other kids as well as family and friends — some who, like you, are here to compete. Others come to cheer and watch the exciting matches.

Find the **score tables**. Here you will see how many points you earn.

Now look at the **mats** where the matches take place! Many are in bright, loud colors like green and red or yellow and blue. Are they similar or different to the mats in your own Jiu Jitsu school?

Did you know?
If you are under 12, your coach or parent is allowed to accompany you and coach you during your match from close-up. They would sit on the chairs near the score tables.

Now look for the **warm-up area**. Move around, strech, jump, roll! Are your muscles ready for the match?

In the **weight-in area**, people will check your weight and examine your Gi to make sure it's the right size and in good condition. If your Gi is too small, you would have an unfair advantage because your opponent would have less material to grab. A Gi with rips or holes might cause an injury if fingers or toes got caught in the holes.

It is exciting to look at the **awards area** with the podium for the medalists. Imagine wearing one of those medals! Will today be your day to win one of these awards?

THE REFEREE

The referee is the boss. What he or she says is law (at least during the match).

The referee wears a **wrist band** on the right hand to represent the fighter who will enter on the right side of the mat. The other hand represents the fighter starting on the left side of the mat. That way the referee can clearly signal whenever a fighter has scored points.

The referee is usually dressed in **black**.

They may seem serious but they are nice people. Their job is to keep things **safe and fair** for you during the match.

They show the points scored with the fingers of their hand:

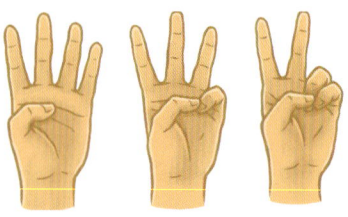

Did you know?
Most of the referees are Blackbelts

THE COMPETION GI

The Gi should be completely **white**, **royal blue** or **black**.

If you are a girl, do not forget to use a stretchy shirt under your Gi.

Once tied in a double knot, each end of the belt should be between 20 and 30 cm.

Use of head gear, hair pins, jewelry or cups (genital protectors) is not allowed!

Did you know?
You can decorate your Gi with cool patches of your academy, sponsors and other fun themes. Just be sure to check with your coach before sewing them on. Patches are only allowed to be added in certain areas on the Gi.

HYGIENE

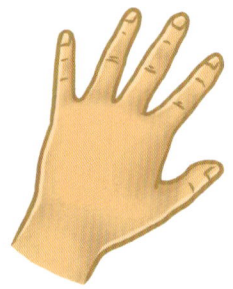 Your fingernails and toenails should be trimmed short so they can't scratch your opponent.

 Long hair must be contained and bound up.

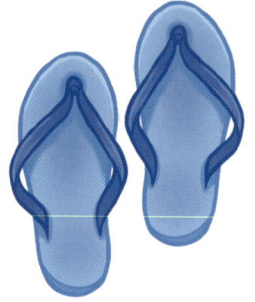 And don't forget to wear your sandals or shoes etc. everywhere to keep those mats clean and bacteria free!

 If you are a girl, you are allowed to cover your head. Just make sure the head covering has no strings or hard materials attached. Don't forget to ask the event organizer which colors are allowed.

 You are not allowed to apply any creams, oils or slippery substances to your body.

 It's ok to be cool but beware! Any hair dye that runs or stains is not allowed!

COMMON WAYS TO WIN

Submission

This is a way to win at any point in the match! This happens when you apply a legal technique that your opponent can't escape. This will cause your opponent to tap at least twice with the hand in order to tell you and the referee that the match is over. When your opponent taps, it's very important to let go of the submission immediately so you don't injure your opponent.

Did you know?
If you can't tap with your hands (maybe they're trapped), then you can use your feet to tap. You can also ask to stop the match. This is called a verbal submission.

Once the match is over, the referee will have both opponents stand and face the scorekeepers, then signals the winner by raising their hand.

Never give up! Even if you are losing by points, you can still win the match at any moment with a submission.

Stoppage

Sometimes, the referee decides to stop the match before the time is over and before anyone has been submitted. This is usually done for reasons of safety. For example, if one fighter tries to armbar their opponent but they refuse to tap, the arm of the opponent risks being stretched too far and injured. The referee will stop it before an injury happens.

Did you know?
If your nose starts to bleed, the referee will stop the match and call for a first aid medic to help stop the bleeding. This can happen two times. If your nose starts bleeding a third time, however, the referee will end the match and award the victory to your opponent.

First aid medics should be present at every tournament in case the athletes need their help. If they aren't, your parents should file a complaint with the organization hosting the event!

For safety during the match, it's important not to resist a submission if you can't escape. To end the match, tap twice right away to let your opponent and the referee know that they should stop it.

Winning by points

When the match time ends but there hasn't been a submission, the fighter with the most points wins. If both fighters have the same number of points (called a draw), then the fighter with the most advantage points wins. If there is a draw in both the number of points and advantage points, the fighter with the lowest penalty points wins.

This position is called mount.

Did you know?
The referee will usually ask the fighters to tie the belts before announcing the winner at the end of the match.

Referee decision

When the match time ends and both fighters have the same number of points, advantage points and penalties points, then the referee will choose the winner.

This position is called closed guard.

A common situation when this happens is closed guard. You are trying to escape, but can't get out of it. Your opponent is trying to sweep or submit you but doesn't succeed either. So, you are both stuck in this position.

Making a decision is not easy for the referee. They need to consider many factors in order to decide who deserves the victory most..

Usually, the most active fighter will be declared the winner. If both fighters are equally active, the fighter with good submission attemps will win over the fighter trying to improve their position.

Disqualification

Sometimes one of the fighters uses a technique or move which is not permitted in the match. These are called fouls.

If the foul is very serious, such as an illegal technique that could cause an injury, then the fighter is disqualified immediately. If the foul is less serious, such as fleeing the bounds of the match area, then the fighter will receive a penalty point. If a fighter gets 4 penalty points, that fighter is disqualified.

The gesture for disqualification is both arms crossed above the referee's head, with fists clenched.

This position is called knee bar and is an example of an illegal technique that leads to immediate disqualification.

If your opponent is disqualified, you will automatically be the winner of the match, no matter how many points were on the scoreboard when it happened.

Did you know?
The referee often uses Brazilian words during the match. For example, "combate" means "begin the fight", and "parou" means "stop".

THE SCORE SYSTEM

There are 7 different positions and actions which can earn you points during the match. These are: Takedown, guard pass, sweep, knee on belly, back-take, mount and back-mount.

The points will be reflected on the scoreboard, next to your name.

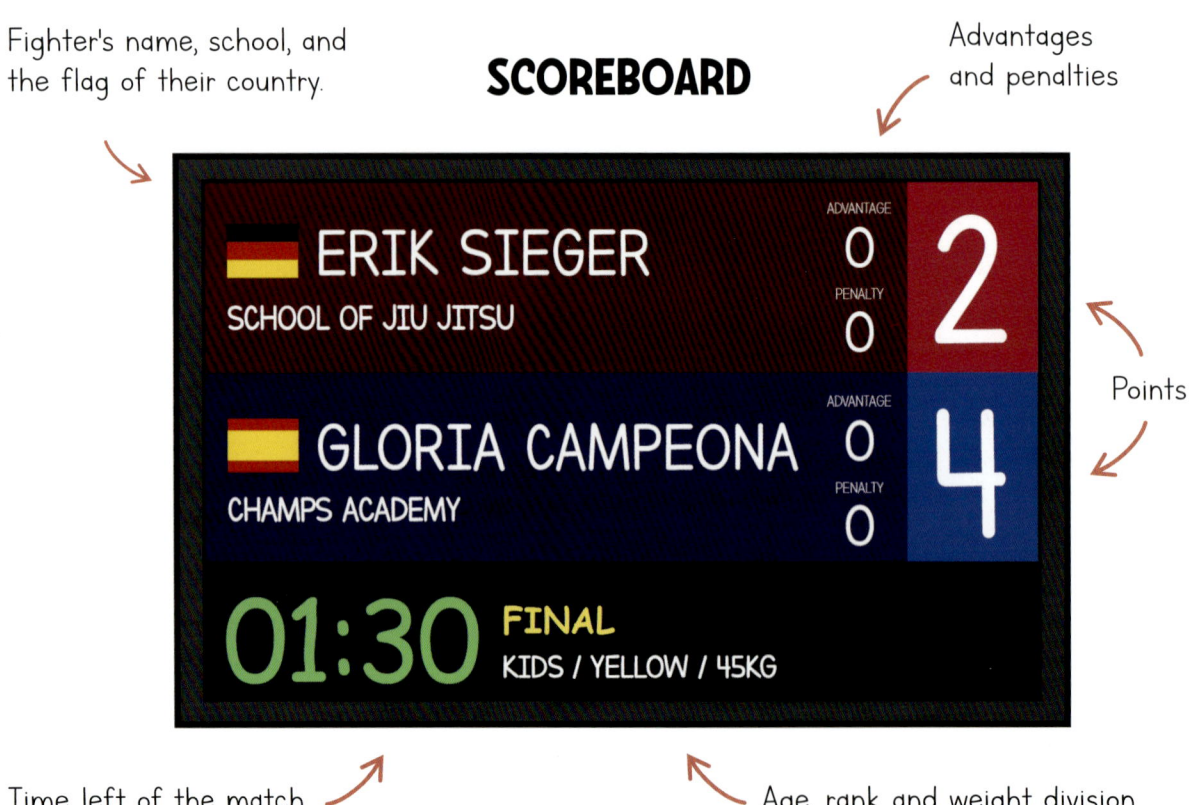

Fighter's name, school, and the flag of their country.

SCOREBOARD

Advantages and penalties

Points

Time left of the match

Age, rank and weight division

A **takedown** happens when you force your opponent to the ground. It doesn't matter if they land on their back, on their side or in a seated position.

A successfull takedown is awarded with **2 points**.

This takedown is called Tai Otoshi.

This position is called Kesa Gatame or side control.

For the takedown to be complete, you must hold top position for at least **3 seconds**.

A **guard pass** happens when you successfullly pass your opponent's guard and reach side control position. A guard is any position where your opponent's legs are between you and their body and block you from reaching the side.

A successfull guard pass is awarded with **3 points**.

This position is called spider guard.

This position is another kind of side control.

For a guard pass to be complete, you must hold side control for at least **3 seconds**.

A **knee on belly** happens when you place a knee on your opponent's belly, chest or ribs while they have their back to the ground or are laying on their side.

A successfull knee on belly is awarded with **2 points**.

The opposite knee can't touch the ground.

Don't forget, your body has to face your opponent's head.

For a knee on belly to be complete, you must hold the position for at least **3 seconds**.

A **mount** or **back-mount** happens when you sit on the opponent's torso with both knees, or one knee and one foot on the ground.

A succesfull mount or back-mount is awarded with **4 points**.

This position is called mount.

This position is called back-mount.

For a mount or back-mount to be complete, you must hold the position for at least **3 seconds**.

A **back-take** happens when you hold your opponent's back and place your heels between their thighs. This foot position is called a hook.

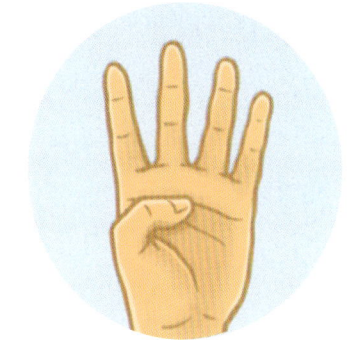

A succesfull back-take is awarded with **4 points**.

Don't forget, your legs should never be crossed in front of your opponent.

For a back-take to be complete, you must hold the position for at least **3 seconds**.

A **sweep** happens when you have your opponent in any kind of guard then, through a serie of movements, you reverse the position so that you are in top position and your opponent is in the bottom position.

A succesfull sweep is awarded with **2 points**.

Did you know?
There are many sweeps in BJJ. This one is called Lumberjack Sweep!

Another kind of sweep happens when you have your opponent in any kind of guard and attempt to reverse the position, but your opponent turns his/her back on all fours. This is called turtle. To get the points for a sweep, you must control the back of your opponent. No hooks are required here.

You can think of a sweep as any kind of attack from the bottom that improves your position.

The bottom position here is called the turtle.

For a sweep to be complete, you must hold top position or the back control for at least **3 seconds**.

ADVANTAGES

When you get close to completing a point-scoring move or a submission but don't quite succeed, then the referee will award you an **advantage point**.

The referee gesture for an advantage point is extending one arm parallel to the mat.

SCOREBOARD

	ERIK SIEGER	ADVANTAGE 0	4
SCHOOL OF JIU JITSU		PENALTY 0	
	GLORIA CAMPEONA	ADVANTAGE 1	4
CHAMPS ACADEMY		PENALTY 0	

00:00 FINAL
KIDS / YELLOW / 45KG

ADVANTAGE
1

Advantage points are shown in the score panel next to the points. These help you to win the match if the score is even!

A common situation where advantage points are scored is when you throw your opponent to the ground (takedown), but they stand up again before you could hold them to the ground for the full 3 seconds.

FOULS

There are 3 kind of fouls: disciplinary, serious and severe fouls.

Disciplinary fouls

They are basically given for bad behavior. When this happens, the referee will stop the match and disqualify the fighter who committed the foul.

Beware! If you commit a disciplinary foul you get disqualified from both the match and the entire competition!

The gesture for disqualification is both arms crossed with fists clenched above the referee's head.

Examples of disciplinary fouls are biting, pulling your opponent's hair, striking, or using bad words or offensive gestures towards your opponent, the referee or spectators.

Did you know?
You can receive a disciplinary foul if you behave badly before or after the match too and not just during the match.

Serious fouls

They happen when you use a technique or move which is not permitted in the match. When this happens, the referee will give you a penalty point.

The referee gesture for a penalty point is a clenched fist held up with the arm bent at shoulder height.

SCOREBOARD

	ERIK SIEGER	ADVANTAGE 0	4
	SCHOOL OF JIU JITSU	PENALTY 0	
	GLORIA CAMPEONA	ADVANTAGE 0	4
	CHAMPS ACADEMY	PENALTY 1	

00:00 FINAL
KIDS / YELLOW / 45KG

PENALTY
1

Penalty points are shown in the score panel next to the points, underneath the advantage points.

When the match ends in a draw, the fighter with the most advantage points wins. If both the number of points and advantage points are equal, the fighter with the lowest number of penalty points wins.

Examples of serious fouls are: leaving the bounds of the match area to avoid the fight, placing a foot or hand in your opponent's face, or jumping to a closed guard on a standing opponent.

In all the divisions for kids under 15 years old, the consequences of serious fouls are as follows:

- 1st serious foul — The referee gives you a penalty point.

- 2nd serious foul — The referee gives you a 2nd penalty point AND gives an advantage point to your opponent.

- 3rd serious foul — The referee gives you a 3rd penalty point AND gives 2 points to your opponent.

- 4th serious foul — The referee gives you a 4th penalty point AND gives 2 more points to your opponent.

- 5th serious foul — The referee gives you a 5th penalty point AND gives 2 more points to your opponent.

- 6th serious foul — The referee disqualifies you from the match.

In all the divisions for teens over 15 years old and adults, the maximum number of penalty points allowed before disqualification is 3.

Did you know?

Lack of combativeness (called stalling) for more than 20 seconds is considered a foul, and has the same consequences as serious fouls described above.

Severe fouls

They happen mostly when you use a technique that is illegal for your age and rank. These moves are forbidden because they are considered too dangerous. If you try to use an illegal technique, the referee will immediately stop the match and disqualify you.

Illegal Moves	Age/Rank				
	4 - 12	13 - 15	16 - 17 (all ranks) & White Belts	Blue & Purple Belts	Brown & Black Belts
Submission streching legs apart	✗	✓	✓	✓	✓
Choke with spinal lock	✗	✗	✓	✓	✓
Straight foot lock	✗	✗	✓	✓	✓
Ezekiel (forearm choke with the sleeve)	✗	✗	✓	✓	✓
Frontal guillotine choke	✗	✗	✓	✓	✓
Omoplata	✗	✗	✓	✓	✓
Triangle (pulling opponent's head down)	✗	✗	✓	✓	✓
Arm triangle	✗	✗	✓	✓	✓
Lock inside the closed guard with legs compressing kidneys or ribs	✗	✗	✗	✓	✓
Wrist lock	✗	✗	✗	✓	✓
Single leg takedown with head on the outside of opponent's body	✗	✗	✗	✓	✓
Biceps slicer	✗	✗	✗	✗	✓

Illegal Moves	Age/Rank				
	4 - 12	13 - 15	16 - 17 (all ranks) & White Belts	Blue & Purple Belts	Brown & Black Belts
Calf slicer	✗	✗	✗	✗	✓
Knee bar	✗	✗	✗	✗	✓
Toe hold	✗	✗	✗	✗	✓
Slam	✗	✗	✗	✗	✗
Spinal lock without choke	✗	✗	✗	✗	✗
Heelhook	✗	✗	✗	✗	✗
Locks twisting the knees	✗	✗	✗	✗	✗
Knee reaping	✗	✗	✗	✗	✗
Scissor takedown	✗	✗	✗	✗	✗
During a straight foot lock, turning in the direction of the foot not under attack	✗	✗	✗	✗	✗
In toe hold, applying outward pressure on the foot	✗	✗	✗	✗	✗
Bending fingers backwards	✗	✗	✗	✗	✗
Grabbing the opponent's belt and throwing them to the floor on his head in defense of a single leg takedown when the opponents head is on the outside of his body	✗	✗	✗	✗	✗
Suplex takedown (landing with the opponent's head or neck on the ground)	✗	✗	✗	✗	✗

Thanks!

AKNOWLEDGEMENTS

This book would have not been possible without the inspiration and support of the BJJ community and the many amazing people I've met through the sport. I am specially grateful to the following Kickstarter backers whose pledges helped to bring this project to life in the early stages of development. Thank you!

- Gloria Molina, my endlessly supportive mother, who's stood by my decisions 100% regardless of how crazy or unconventional they might seem.

- Mercedes (Moqui) Ramírez, my little sister, who could easily be a blackbelt but has chosen to pursue other endeavors. Such a waste of talent for the BJJ world!

- Tony Hesse, my partner in crime and love of my life. Blackbelt and co-owner of Nexus Fighter Academy, Hamburg (Germany).

- Stefan Giersch, eternal white belt but blackbelt in friendship, of Nexus Fighter Academy, Hamburg (Germany)

- Danny Mitchel, blackbelt 2nd Degree, of AVT MMA Leeds, Leeds (United Kingdom)

- Jeane Ruiz

- Constanze Genko, mum of the dragon and purple belt, of Ataque Duplo BJJ Association e.V, Hannover (Germany)

- Juan Antonio Mermarzadeh, grey-black belt, of Nexus Fighter Academy, Hamburg (Germany)

- Gabriel Mermarzadeh, grey belt of Nexus Fighter Academy, Hamburg (Germany)

- Laurien & Alex Zurhake, purple belts, great people, owners and coaches of Team Laurien & Alex, Munich (Germany)

- Jan Christiaan Herbert, black belt 1st degree of Sportschool Herber, Ede, (Netherlands)

LEARNING ACTIVITIES

The following section includes a few fun and learning activities about BJJ.

Visit bjjtherulesofthegame.com to view or download the answer key.

Tip: You can make copies of these pages instead of writing directly in your book. This way, you can enjoy the activities multiple times!

These fun activities are sponsored by

Word search

Below are 10 names of BJJ positions and techniques. How many of them can you find in the letter box below?

Mount   Takedown   Sweep   Guard   Armbar
Lumberjack   Ezekiel   Backtake   Sidecontrol   Choke

L	O	E	R	E	E	C	W	O	R	E	D	D	U
D	K	T	A	E	N	H	A	I	U	A	O	G	A
E	A	M	C	S	W	E	E	P	H	C	L	U	Z
A	Z	U	G	O	M	A	R	M	B	A	R	A	L
E	D	C	I	U	E	O	D	K	O	L	S	R	N
A	E	L	Z	R	O	W	U	E	B	N	K	D	S
E	K	A	T	K	C	A	B	A	G	K	R	M	K
U	O	O	B	N	H	U	E	C	A	M	O	B	S
T	T	G	I	C	K	T	P	Z	D	K	N	E	J
M	O	U	N	T	R	G	E	C	E	H	S	I	A
A	O	U	R	G	B	A	C	P	H	K	G	B	S
A	N	W	O	D	E	K	A	T	C	O	I	N	E
G	K	C	A	J	R	E	B	M	U	L	K	E	D
S	I	D	E	C	O	N	T	R	O	L	E	E	L

Find the differences

Can you find 10 differences between these two pictures?

Find the technique

Erik and Gloria are training hard for their next tournament! Follow the lines from the fighters to the techniques they have been practicing, and write those in the box next to each fighter.

Gloria has learned the following techniques:

CLOSED GUARD

KNEE ON BELLY

BACK-MOUNT

KESA GATAME

GUARD PASS

Erik has learned the following techniques:

TURTLE

42

Match the pictures

Draw a line connecting the images of techniques and positions on the left to the corresponding referee gestures and point values on the right.

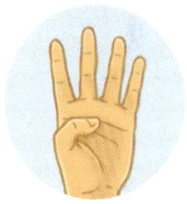

Coloring page

Crossword puzzle

Complete the crossword by filling in the word that fits each clue.

Across
2. The Brazilian word that means „start the fight".
4. The panel where the competition points are shown.
6. A forearm choke using the sleeve, forbidden for kids under 15 years old.
7. A metal disc with words or a picture on it, given as a reward for winning a competition.
8. The number points you get when you successfully sweep your opponent.

Down
1. A BJJ guard which has the name of a tiny animal that makes webs.
3. The number of seconds you need to hold any position in order to get the points.
5. The darkest allowed in competition Gis.
7. The position when you sit on your opponent's torso with both knees touching the ground.

Advanced learners quiz

1. How many seconds do you need to hold a position in order to receive points for having successfully completed it?

    A. 4 seconds

    B. 3 seconds

    C. 3 minutes

2. If you were successful with a takedown and landed in the mount position, how many points would you receive?

    A. 6 points

    B. 2 points

    C. 4 points

3. If you applied a good armbar, but your opponent defended well and was able to escape, what points would you receive?

    A. 0 points

    B. 1 advantage point

    C. 1 point

4. You are a yellow belt entering an IBJJF tournament. Are you allowed to use leg locks?

    A. No.

    B. Yes, always.

    C. Yes, but only if you have trained them before in the gym.

5. While applying a choke, your opponent bites you! What will the referee do?

    A. Stop the match, and disqualify your opponent from the match.

    B. Stop the match, ask your opponent politely not to do it again, then resume the match.

    C. Stop the match, and disqualify your opponent from the entire competition.

6. Which of the following statements is true for IBJJ tournaments?

    A. Both boys and girls can cover their heads.

    B. Girls can cover their head as long as no strings or hard pieces are attached.

    C. Girls can cover their head any way they like.

7. You are entering an IBJJF tournament. Which are the official colours for a competition Gi?

    A. White, red and royal blue.

    B. White, black and navy blue.

    C. White, black and royal blue.

Building your game plan

It's good to have a game plan! Use the boxes below to create a list of techniques when you are in the following positions. There are not right and wrong answers. This exercise for advanced learners will help you think about your options and define your own style.

Starting a match standing

In opponent's closed guard

I have a closed guard

On top of side control

In opponent's open guard

I have an open guard

On bottom of side control

My back is taken

I am mounted

I have the mount

I have the back

Draw your own BJJ picture

Use the space below to create your own BJJ picture! Need some ideas? What about drawing yourself on the podium, or drawing your favorite Gi?

Another idea would be to draw a picture of what a kid's class look like at your academy. Draw anything you'd like, as long as it relates to BJJ.